G000112042

LONDON:
BEHIND THE STATUES

ALISON HASLAM

An A-Z of behind the scenes facts
about London's statues

Photographs by Irena Wojnarowska

BLITHFIELD PUBLISHING

Why Statues?

This book is a collection of many light-hearted tales and amusing anecdotes about some of London's famous statues and the colourful characters they represent.

These statues are scattered all over London – on street corners, in garden squares and tucked away in niches. The more famous ones are on top of columns, the lesser known ones hidden from view. However, who they are and what they have done to deserve a place in history, let alone on a plinth, remains, to most of us a mystery. They are just there, static, mute and seemingly irrelevant.

So in order to inject a breath of fresh air into these overlooked street ornaments, whose only common link is fame, I thought it would be fun to dig a little deeper to see if there was anything vaguely interesting or amusing about them – there was plenty!

For than reason alone, I decided, that instead of just concentrating on all their worthy achievements, which of course are interesting, but a tad dull, I would give you what you really want to know – all the scandal, gossip and mishaps!

So, packed to the gills with historic yet facetious and amusing facts, I have selected some of my favourite stories relating to these statues, in an attempt to bring each one back to life and to give you a whole new outlook on some of the Nation's greatest!

DEDICATION
To Frank, whose annoying insistence "You can do it Alison!"
finally inspired me

A IS FOR:

Achilles, according to Greek mythology was the bravest Greek warrior in the decade long Trojan War, and therefore assumed to be the perfect role model on which to base our own Napoleonic hero, Arthur Wellesley, The Duke of Wellington, also known, on account of his big nose, as Beaky.

Victorious in his defeat of Napoleon and the French in the 1815 Battle of Waterloo, the Duke became a national hero. So to celebrate his success on the battlefield, we erected several statues of him, three of which, show him mounted on his trusty steed, the unpopular Copenhagen. A vicious little mare, greatly disliked for her nasty habit of delivering hind-leg kicks to the unsuspecting and also, the only horse in history to be buried with full military honours.

The number of statues of the Duke outnumbers those of any monarch to date, which indicates his popularity at the time. One of these double acts is in the City, another in St. Paul's Cathedral, the third in the country, and the fourth one is opposite his former home, Apsley House, which was given to him as a gift from a 'Grateful Nation', and boasts the best address of No.1 London.

This statue, however, is drastically different from all the others - no horse, no likeness and as far as the Duke was concerned – No Comment! Plus, it is cast from the unusual source of captured French canons. These were brought back, melted down and then expertly

reconfigured into Achilles, by the sculptor Richard Westmacott, whose mythological representation of the Duke was perfectly in tune with that of the 'Grateful Ladies of Great Britain'. A group of which, whom having raised the necessary funds for the statue, through public subscription, were utterly delighted with the result.

Achilles, now complete and ready to impress the world at large, was transported over to Hyde Park, then encircled by railings, at which point plans to erect the statue came to an abrupt halt. The railings, at the time, were interspersed with small pedestrian gate-ways, one of which was intended for Achilles' 'admittance for admiration', but as no one had thought to check on either his or the gateways vital statistics, it was a tad embarrassing, at this crucial stage, to discover their obvious incompatibility. So, until workmen were able to widen the gap, Achilles' erection and the eagerly awaited unveiling ceremony were both unavoidably held-up. Eventually the 18ft statue made its way through to his allocated spot, where it was cemented into place, and minus his fig leaf, (added at a later stage), was finally presented to the nation!

As for the unveiling ceremony itself, it was by all accounts a riotous affair, attended by the Dukes female fans, who flocked in their hundreds on the day, all keen to be a part of the proceedings. Unlike the Duke himself, whom, to his credit, remained mute on the subject and absent on the day. A marked contrast to the behaviour of three of his keener fans, who broke free from rank, tradition and protocol in their determined efforts to get closer to their hero. Overcome by all the excitement, two of them had a stroke, the third one couldn't reach and as a result of this unprecedented display of affection, the statue was immediately dubbed 'The Ladies Trophy!'

Hyde Park/Park Lane – Richard Westmacott, erected 1822

7

B IS FOR:

Queen **Boudicea** of the Iceni was the famous red-haired Queen who mounted a successful rebellion against the Romans, in retaliation for an earlier attack on her tribe, who once lived in the county of Norfolk.

Back in the not so good old days of 61 AD the Romans, who occupied the country, at the time, reneged on their usual arrangements with one of their client King's. The one in question was the recently deceased King Prasutagas, whose widow Boudicca, was then, taken madly advantage of, by them, as they ruthlessly set about relieving her of all of her land and possessions, in an unprovoked and unforgivable attack.

Instead of sticking to their usual custom of only taking their fair share, they decided to seize all of Boudicca's portion as well, which was then followed up by a humiliating and gratuitous show of violence, rape and pillage, culminating in a forceful whipping for those few still left standing.

As neither Boudicca, nor her two daughters were exempt from this attack and show of manpower, she decided to avenge her husbands' rights and wishes and give the Romans a dose of their own medicine.

Clearly a revolt was the answer, and taking the opportunity of the absent London Governor, the Iceni army, led by their Queen, rode south to London for revenge.

Westminster Bridge – Thomas Thornycroft, unveiled 1902

Their journey was broken up along the way for two practise runs, the first one took place in Colchester and the second in St. Albans, where, unstoppable by the few remaining Roman soldiers, who were taken unawares by these attacks, they swiftly razed both cities to the ground.

With two down and one to go, the Iceni, heady with smell of sweet success in the air, albeit mixed, with the not so sweet smell of burning pyres, headed on to Londinium, their third and final destination, which was also quickly reduced to a sea of ash.

The news of all this havoc relayed itself fairly rapidly over to Wales, where the Roman Governor, Suetonius Paulinus, who had been rather busy suppressing their revolt, found himself forced to put them on hold and rush back to town. On arrival, he was utterly dismayed to find things not quite as he had left them. His legions and cities now lay in waste and with an estimated 70,000 fatalities things were looking fairly grim.

They weren't looking all that good for Boudicca either, who, well aware that the Romans would not rest until her capture and inevitable death, took matters into her own hands and outwitted the Romans one more time, by drinking from a poisoned phial and committing suicide.

Her armies keen to leave the scene of the crime, headed northeast together with their dead Queen, only stopping briefly to bury her in the open fields of north London. This part of town is nowadays home to British Rail's King's Cross Station, which ironically is the terminus used for Norfolk bound passengers and where Boudicca is allegedly buried, in an unmarked grave, underneath Platform 10!

Houses of Parliament – Sir William Hamo Thornycroft 1899

IS FOR:

Oliver **Cromwell** styled himself as Lord Protector of England following his successful outcome of the civil war and the ultimate disposal of King Charles I. After this, for the first time ever, the country was without a monarch and Cromwell's eleven-year 'reign' is referred to as the Inter-regnum.

His no-nonsense and Puritanical approach came as a huge shock to the public as he quickly set about laying down the law. First to go were the theatres, which were closed down, along with the dogfights, bear baits and, of course, all other forms of gambling. The big shock came when he banned Christmas, then the game of Tennis, after which public monuments, then deemed to be idolatrous, were trashed and destroyed.

The very fact that we even have a statue of him at all, given his history, is pretty extraordinary, and even more remarkable is how and where he ended up!

His statue, which stands in front of Westminster Hall, the same place where Charles I stood trial, was paid for (anonymously) by Lord Rosebery, a former Prime Minister. His attempts to persuade Parliament to pay for the statue fell on deaf ears, so he ended up paying for it himself, and also chose the site where it now stands. It shows Cromwell wearing his spurs, which happen to be upside-down, and gazing across the road into the eyes of his old adversary, King Charles, whose miniature bust is tucked away in a little niche above a doorway of St. Margaret's Church, the parish church for members of both the Houses of Commons and Lords. It is rather is the shadows of Westminster Abbey, which is where he was buried, albeit for just three years which we will come back to in a moment.

Cromwell died exactly seven years after winning the decisive Battle of Worcester in 1651, which forced Charles II to flee the country, the Scots to go back home, but most importantly, reinforced the Commonwealth, with Cromwell himself declaring the successful outcome of this Royalist attack to be a 'crowning mercy'. However, just before battle commenced, he disappeared for a few moments, which were accounted for in a rather strange and spooky tale.

There are two versions of the same story, and although both, allegedly, took place in separate locations, the content and outcome are exactly the same. Backed up by independent witnesses they relate how Cromwell met and made a pact with the Devil – this victory in return for his life! Cromwell was overheard arguing with a 'black hooded stranger', who remained adamant in denying Cromwell's requests. His first, for 21 years was turned down and the second one, amended to 14, was also refused. The only offer forthcoming was a seven-year deal, or nothing, and Cromwell, hell-bent (as it turned out) on winning, agreed to these terms. The deed was done, the battle was won and sure enough, exactly seven years later on 30th November 1658, at 3 pm, the Devil claimed his soul!

Back at Westminster Abbey, Cromwell had himself buried, with great aplomb, in the illustrious Henry VII Chapel, but as the plaque

12

clearly indicates he was only there until 1661. This date more or less coincides with the restoration of Charles II, which was a good thing for the monarchy who've stayed in place ever since, but not so good for Cromwell, who didn't! The new King was about to have his revenge. He had his father's 'murderer' dug up, removed from the Royal Church and posthumously given a traditional traitors send-off!

Back then, the usual means of disposal for common thieves and

felons was the barbaric yet conclusive and effective method of hanging, drawing and quartering, which was exactly what happened to Cromwell. After his decomposed body was removed from the Abbey, it spent the night in Red Lion Square, supposedly still haunted by his ghost. The following morning the corpse was sent to Tyburn, where it was hung from the gibbet and after wards, what was left of his mortal remains, were flung unceremoniously into a pit. Apart from the skull, which was saved for the grotesque finale! This was then rammed upon a pole and displayed upon the roof of Westminster Hall, where it remained, impaled, for the best part of twenty years!

Finally, due to a huge gust of wind one stormy night, it came unstuck from its' anchoring after which it somehow managed to be rescued and retrieved, eventually ending up back at Cromwell's former university college, where, in the archives of Sidney Sussex College, Cambridge, it still remains!

13

D IS FOR:

David – was the Biblical hero who catapulted into the limelight after slaying the mighty giant Goliath, with his nifty use of stone and sling, which made him the perfect choice for the Machine Gun Corps to base their First World War Memorial upon and didn't they have good taste!

This David, who was made from Mazzona marble, wins, without contest, 'The Best Bottom in London' award, was expertly sculpted by Francis Derwent White. He stands in the round, with Goliath's sword in one hand and on top of his plinth which is wedged in-between two Vickers's machine-guns supporting their own wreaths. The statue is a fabulous fusion of style and stance, echoing both Michelangelo's and Donatello's versions of David, whose casts are on display within the plaster courts at the Victoria and Albert Museum, in South Kensington.

The statue was unveiled in 1925 by the Duke of Connaught, who was invited to officiate at the ceremony, which subsequently, but not surprisingly, attracted a lot more attention than the average war memorial was used to. However, in David's case, not all of it was welcome.

It soon transpired that not everyone was in favour of being confronted by a full frontal nude in the morning, especially on the way to work! Which was what the very proper and formidable members of the 'Women's Society of

14

Purity' strenuously objected to. The main problem, as they saw it, was his positioning, which initially faced Park Lane, thus greeting all of its' oncoming traffic together with the hundreds of commuters and shoppers, whose daily journey took them right past him. The public were nonchalant about the nude, their thoughts, no doubt, wholly occupied with the solemnity of its' representation. However, it rankled enough with the worthy sisters of the WSOP who insisted upon its' removal.

15

In their opinion, it was inappropriate, obscene and downright disgusting, and on that basis, they launched a campaign against the council demanding action. The council however, in their infinite wisdom, refused to take the ladies complaint seriously and like the Machine Gun Corp, stuck rigidly to their guns and remained equally resolute. At this point, with all parties locked in verbal combat a solution seemed unlikely, until some bright spark came up with the best suggestion yet, "How about just turning him around?"

It was the most perfect compromise. London kept its memorial, neither party lost face and David, continued to uphold the Biblical example, and turned the other cheek!

Hyde Park Corner – Francis Derwent Wood, unveiled 1925

E IS FOR:

Eros

Right in the middle of Piccadilly Circus, once known as the Centre of the Empire, is The Shaftesbury Memorial, which was erected to commemorate the life and works of Anthony Ashley Cooper, the 7th Earl of Shaftesbury, who was a Victorian philanthropist, Christian and reformer.

The winged archer on top of the memorial, shown balancing on one foot, is commonly, but incorrectly known as Eros. Ironically an inappropriate mistake, as this messenger is none other than the Angel of Christian Charity, put there to reflect Shaftesbury's moral principles and beliefs which differ enormously to those of Eros, who is the pagan God of Love.

In fact everything to do with this monument, from its name and position, down to its size and inscription contradict the well-meaning intentions of the man it commemorates.

Lord Shaftesbury, was famous for his reforms within the factories and mines, which made him as popular with the masses as unpopular with the establishment, making him as unique then as his monument is today.

Particularly so, as it supports the only aluminium statue in London,

16

Piccadilly Circus – Alfred Gilbert

the Angel, which also happens to be facing the wrong way! This mistake occured after it had been taken down for cleaning and now, instead of facing Shaftesbury Avenue, a street littered with theatres, which takes its name from the Earl, has its back to it. The making and naming of this street is also, in itself ironic, as it completely destroyed row upon row of slums, homes to the very people he had worked tirelessly to protect.

As for the inscription, this can be found around its base and like all inscriptions, extols the virtues and values of the said honored man. However, this over-elaborate and flowery one has a bit of a sting in its tale, not because of the words which really do reflect well on Shaftesbury, but because of its author, the then Prime Minister, William Gladstone who happened to be his most bitter political opponent.

Finally, we come to the very structure itself, which also didn't turn out as intended. The architect, Sir Alfred Gilbert was given the task of designing the monument, which unexpectedly and half way through the planning stages had its budget drastically slashed, leaving Sir Alfred with no other choice, than to dramatically scale down the size of the fountain basin, The reduced basin, now unable to cope with the force of water simply spewed forth, soaking anyone unlucky enough to be passing. The general public and the press, were under-whelmed and poor Alfred, unable to cope with the negative publicity, upped sticks and fled the country.

He was followed in due course by his own creation, Eros, who also ended up leaving town for a while. His departure, however, was based on concerns for his own safety. So for the duration of World War II, he swapped his pivotal role in town for a much quieter one in the country, living life under wraps down in the Berkshire town of Egham, as a wartime evacuee!

F IS FOR:

Charles James **Fox** – The fantastic Mr. Fox was without a doubt, the most unconventional politician we have ever had. Whose predilection for gambling, women and politics, in that specified order, established him as one of our most entertaining politicians and guaranteed him a well deserved place in history. He even began his political career illegally, under-aged at twenty, when he became the Liberal Member of Parliament for Midhurst, his ticket into Parliament!

CJ, as he became known, rapidly made a name for himself on the benches, with his clever and erudite speeches, regularly outwitting and infuriating both the members of the opposition and the government by challenging their ideas, policies and ideals. His unique viewpoint was severely at odds with those of the establishment, including King George III and William Pitt, the Prime Minister, whose ideas on the main issues of the day, i.e. Napoleon and both the French and American Revolutions, greatly differed from his.

Unsurprisingly, these little maverick ways of his, had an adverse affect on his career. Marked by his all time low, at Parliament, which arrived at the same time as his cab. This was rather handy, as it managed to take him and all the other members of the opposition home, so few were they in numbers! In contrast to this, he did manage to secure a resolution to abolish slavery, which was achieved just before he died. After which he was buried in the aptly named Radicals Corner, at Westminster Abbey and along side his old political sparring opponent, the former Prime Minister, William Pitt.

But life wasn't all work, as away from the daily world of politics, CJ was quick to resume and pursue his other passion, gambling, for which

18

Bloomsbury Square – Sir Richard Westmacott 1816

he and his all night stints became as legendary as his liberal views.

What man the man so remarkable, was his amazing ability and stamina, that enabled him to debate all day at the Commons and gamble all night at his club, the latter less successfully so as he was also famous

for losing spectacular amounts of money! One such occasion being, the night when he and his brother between them, lost a staggering £32,000. Unperturbed, by the loss, he played on, his gambling habit made all the more easier by the plentiful supply of money, forthcoming from either the waiters, who were happy to lend small amounts or the Jewish money lenders, delighted to lend the larger ones. They were also happy to wait up all night, if need be, for repayment in a downstairs anteroom at Brooks', which became dubbed, the 'Jerusalem Chamber' on account of their frequent visits.

As both activities took up so much of his time, there was precious little of it left for the basics, such as washing, shaving or even changing clothes. So most days he would go straight back to the Commons after a nights' play, his wits sharpened and honed, ready to begin his 'day job' all over again!

Yet despite his dishevelled state, he had quite a following among the ladies, one of which was the gorgeous Georgiana, The Duchess of Devonshire. She, on account of her unconventional marriage, had quite a bit of extra time on her hands, which she put to good use, when canvassing on behalf of CJ, for a local election. She did this by promising kisses in return for Liberal votes, which is something quite unheard of in this day and age, but nevertheless, was fairly successful.

This unique method of securing the vote was then taken up and developed by another unlikely source, 'Honest Sam', a Soho publican. He took the idea one step further and offered free pints at his pub in return for votes and at the same time renamed it 'The Intrepid Fox'. A perfect tribute to this maverick politician.

IS FOR:

George IV – reigned as King of England for just ten years, from 1820 to 1830 after succeeding his father 'mad' King George III.

This George, as his title suggests, was the fourth George to reign in slow succession, after the first one took up the reins in 1714, when the heirless Queen Anne died, and, if truth be told, they were all a bit of a funny lot!

Each generation passed down, amongst other unattractive traits, their inbred hatred for their sons, much in the same way that the early ones passed down their mistresses to the next of kin, thus provoking the newspapers to raise and answer their own salacious question:

"Is there nothing new under the sun?"

"No" came the reply, "Nor under the grandson!"

Although this George thankfully didn't have one, it did not stop him from transferring this loathsome family characteristic onto his wife, by dumping her the moment their daughter was born, offering her £50,000 to stay out of the country and banning her from his Coronation.

Their marriage, it has to be said, was not a huge success, partially due to the couple themselves and also the way in which the whole thing had been brought about. Up until the time of this marriage, Prinny, the perennial King-in-Waiting had been having the time of his life, and as he had no serious role to play, simply decided to play more seriously by devoting himself to a life of sheer self-indulgence, par excellence. His love affairs were as numerous as his debts were insurmountable, and finally, when both appeared to be spiralling out of control, his father, aided by the government, intervened. Fed up with

21

George and his errant ways, exacerbated by his lavish spending, loose morals and debauched way of life, plus his debts, which topped an astronomical £650,000, and had no way of being paid of, they presented him with their master plan. An arranged marriage in return for becoming debt free. Unpalatable as it seemed on the one hand, it proved irresistible on the other, and George, now in no position to argue, reluctantly accepted.

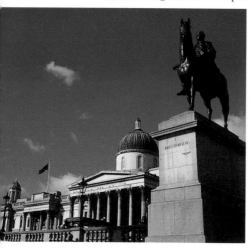

He had already annoyed his father by secretly marrying the actress Mrs Marie Fitzherbert, which the King, promptly annulled with his trump card – the Royal Marriage Act. This, forbade members of the Royal family to marry without the consent of the monarch, if under 25, or to a Roman Catholic. All of which, well and truly put the kybosh on love's young dream, as George then found himself in breach of the Act, on all three counts.

Trafalgar Square – Sir Francis Chantry

This time, his chosen bride, albeit not by him, was Caroline of Ansbach, whose first meeting and subsequent marriage was preceded by a very special and unusual gift, that he was simply unable to appreciate. It came in the unusual form of a tooth, which happened to be one of hers, especially selected and extracted for him as a 'token of her affection'. This, followed by Caroline, met for the first time in the flesh, proved all too much for George, and unable to make a recovery from either the tooth of its' owner, turned to his emissary saying "Get me out of here, I feel unwell".

Their wedding night saw George, drunk and asleep in the fire-grate, and within a year of being married, their duty done having produced their only child, the couple parted. George, who had never really left his bachelor way of life, upped the ante with his friends, spending more time with CJ Fox, the gambler and politician and Beau Brummel, the dandy, trendsetter and socialite. This friendship, like so many of his, inevitably went pear-shaped after a rift, which became unsalvageable after Beau saw his former friend walking arm-in-arm with a new one, and unable to resist a dig at the Prince's tubby figure, maliciously enquired of the new companion "Who's your fat friend?"

Eventually, this Prince of W(h)ales, became King and as he intended living at Buckingham Palace, began renovations. As he also required a smart entrance, he commissioned his friend and architect John Nash and the sculptor Sir Francis Chantry, to design one and between them, they came up with Marble Arch and his equestrian statue.

For the first time ever, George found himself firmly mounted, which again was a short-lived existence that came to an end after his death, and his niece's ascension to the throne. Queen Victoria, who hated anything to do with her 'wicked uncle' soon set about dismantling and removing the 'eyesore', by having the pair lifted and separated. The arch was sent north, to what has now become an area known as Marble Arch, and as for George, he was dispatched to Trafalgar Square. Where he still remains, on a pigeon-ridden plinth, foot-loose, due to his lack of stirrups and fancy free!

IS FOR:

William **Huskisson** – was the President of the Board of Trade and the Member of Parliament for Liverpool. But much more importantly and the whole reason for including him, is his real claim to fame – he was the first man to be knocked over and killed by a train!

This fatal accident occurred on 15th September 1830 when he was invited, in his official capacity as MP, up to Liverpool, to open the new railway line to Manchester. The whole event was one of great excitement, not only was there to be a new branch line, but this was the debut run for the latest locomotive, the 'Rocket', which, guaranteed to go at least 30mph, had attracted virtually every train spotter in the country.

Huskisson, well aware of the momentous occasion, stood forward to make his speech. He cut the ribbon, then pronounced the line well and truly open, after-which came his big mistake. He crossed back over the tracks and had the misfortune to be run over by another train, after being knocked to the ground by one of its doors, which, had chosen that exact moment to swing open.

Moments later and still wearing his top hat, he was heard to murmur, "I have met my death", and he was right, as it was indeed the sorry case. Amongst others who witnessed the event, was the Duke of Wellington, who utterly loathed the man and declared the whole accident to be "A true act of God"!

After his death, the sculptor John Gibson was given the task of immortalising the man, which he did by portraying him as a Roman Emperor. At least it would appear so, on the basis of the unusual choice of garment chosen for Huskisson, which is a toga. This apparently had more to do with the sculptor's dislike of frock coat and trousers and less to do with any preconceived ideas of grandeur, classical aspirations or associations of this former MP.

However, his misadventures continued to haunt him beyond the grave, as once his statue was completed, his wife then donated it onto

Pimlico Gardens – John Gibson 1836

Lloyds of London. They, in turn, only accepted it because they rated the sculptor and not the man or his deeds. So on that basis they allowed him to decorate their foyer, until a redecoration programme, deemed him surplus to requirements. After which, he was donated yet again, this time to London's County Council, who popped him over to Pimlico gardens, where he still remains in place, but sadly, not exempt from public ridicule. Shortly after arriving in Pimlico, Osbert Sitwell, an amusing man of his day, noticed Huskisson's head struggling to emerge through the swirling mists, caused by the nearby River Thames, and used his acerbic wit rather well to describe him as, "Boredom rising from the bath".

25

IS FOR:

Henry **Irving** was christened plain old John Henry Bodribb, and after having the good sense to change his name, went on to achieve fame and fortune as a leading Victorian actor, famous for his Shakespearian roles. He is also the only actor represented by a statue in London and the first one to be rewarded with a knighthood, which he initially turned down!

He declared himself to be above all such honours, his talent, he assured us, was simply enough. It was a worthy and commendable decision after all he wasn't the first, nor the last to turn such an honour down. At the time, the gesture was seen as ground breaking and won him extra points among his fellow thespians, for his proletarian ways. However, twelve years down the line and long after all the fuss had died down, he had a sudden change of heart and mind and decided to accept it after all. Luckily for him, the palace had not changed their mind and shortly after the u-turn had been approved, Mr. Bodribb, was invited to kneel before the King, knighted, in the time-honoured fashion and arose as, Sir Henry Irving.

Like any true professional, he performed to the very end, which in his case was during a performance of Tennyson's play Becket. When shortly after proffering up the fatal line "Into thy hands O Lord…" Henry, just as Thomas had done before him, passed on, albeit without the aid of four ruthless Knights.

To mark his birthday on the 11th February, the Irving Society lay a wreath on the head of 'The Elevator of the Stage', a worthy nickname, on account of his height, which also causes a problem for those intent on continuing this tradition.

Charing Cross Road – Sir Thomas Brock, unveiled 1910

From the looks of things this year, they have taken the easier option of laying a wreath at his feet, whereas on previous anniversaries, the Society, have had to resort to using either stepladders or stools, to achieve their aim. All of which, goes to make the whole ceremony a rather tricky and precarious one, especially on one memorable year, when neither prop was available. This forced the society to improvise, which, like all good actors they managed to do rather well, the net result being a slightly cock-eyed wreath for Sir Henry, which made its way rather unceremoniously onto his head, courtesy of a tall volunteer and a golf umbrella!

J

IS FOR:

Dr Edward **Jenner** was an army surgeon and county doctor, whose fantastic discovery of using cowpox as a vaccine against smallpox, saved the nation from disaster. He was the first to notice, during his investigations into the disease, that farm workers and milkmaids, working with cows never contracted it, which started him thinking and eventually led him on to his discovery.

His first vaccine was given on 14th May 1796, to a brave boy called James Phipps who, survived not only the trauma of the injection, but all future attempts of re-infection with smallpox. As with all new ideas, it was met with initial resistance, but after this

28

Kensington Gardens – W Calder Marshall

successful experiment, the vaccine, its approval, the treatment and funds to develop it, were all swift in forthcoming.

The word 'vaccination' is also accredited to Dr Jenner for inventing it, which comes from the Latin word 'Vacca' meaning cow, and was later adopted by Louis Pasteur who popularised it, if that is at all possible, as a word used for immunization against any disease.

Thirty-five years after his death, in 1832, Dr Jenner's statue was erected in Trafalgar Square. The arrival of this medical man broke with tradition and marked a change on the London statue scene, which up until then had mainly confined itself to monarchs and military men. However, as a sign of public recognition and the nations gratitude for his life-changing discovery, he was rewarded, not only with a place in history but one on a plinth as well, together with our other national hero's.

Four short years later, however, Dr Jenner found himself up-ended and relocated to the relative backwater of Kensington Gardens, his original place in Trafalgar Square now needed for a more up-to-date and higher profile occupant, and whilst Jenner seemed content to stare at the fountains of the Italianate Water Gardens, which his new home provided, the satirical magazine Punch had their own take on events. Once this move had caught their the attention, they were quick to pen the line:

"I saved you from many spots, shame they couldn't save one for me"

Then followed it up by the equally pertinent question:

"Surely the inventor of vaccinations has the best possible right to make experiments on various spots?"

K IS FOR:

King Charles I the only King in British history to be publicly executed yet still manages to cut sway among a certain group of society. They, are a keen band of Royalists, called the Sealed Knot whom with great solemnity, detail and dedication re-enact the Kings final journey from the Mall, by St. James's Palace, down to the Banqueting House in Whitehall, which, for the King, took place on a cold winters day, on 30th January 1649.

These days, their procession takes place on the Sunday closest to this actual date, when they all gather on the Mall, wearing traditional costumes and armour and carrying weaponry of the day. Once the signal is given, they make their way silently along the Mall, accompanied only by the sound of a solitary beating drum, which makes the whole spectacle incredibly moving and evocative, and the atmosphere becomes charged with surreal anticipation. On arrival at the Banqueting House, they pause for a brief ceremony before moving up to Trafalgar Square, where they lay a wreath at the base of his statue. Behind which is the exact centre of London, from where all distances to and from the capital are measured.

The Sealed Knot's attention to detail is exceptional and through this very simply yet dramatic ceremony they ensure that we continue to revere the King and his last word – REMEMBER!

The main reason that this dinky 5ft 2in King ended up the way he did, was because of his wholehearted and firm belief in the Divine Right of Kings, which differed tremendously to those of Parliament, led by the strong willed puritan Oliver Cromwell. This resulted in the country being plummeted into its' only Civil War which began in 1642.

Seven years later, the victory was Cromwell's and after Charles I's execution, he ruled the country for the following eleven years. After his death, his son Richard attempted to take over, but lacking in all his fathers' leadership qualities, he soon sank without trace. His only legacy is the Cromwell Road, one of London's main arterial roads, which apparently he lived close to. Fortunately for us, it took his surname and

Trafalgar Square – Hubert le Sueur 1633

not his nickname, the rather apt 'Tumble Down Dick'!

After him, came the Restoration, yippee! Charles II was invited back from France, where he had been living in exile, and life returned back to normal. As for the statue, this has it own unusual tale to tell, and as far as stories go, this one really takes the biscuit! After Cromwell had taken charge, he naturally wanted to rid himself of any reminders of the former King, especially this equestrian statue. It was sculpted by the Frenchman Hubert le Seuer, who cannily engraved his own initials on one of the horse's front hooves. So, in order to remove and destroy it, Cromwell employed the services of a local brazier, John Rivett. He undertook the task in hand with great relish, and far as everyone was concerned, had it broken down and melted. He also went on to make a tidy profit from selling souvenirs and trinkets made from the metal, fashioned into knife-handles and other desirable objects. However, after Charles's restoration, the brazier paid a visit to the King, to inform him that the statue of his dad was actually still intact. As he, a true blue

Royalist, had kept it, hidden, and out of view for the last eleven years, having safely buried it at the bottom of his garden!

Charles was naturally delighted by the news and rewarded him handsomely for his efforts. Then, re-erected his father's statue on the exact spot where his enemies had plotted his downfall, facing towards Whitehall, which also, sadly, happened to be his.

Another small yet permanent reminder of these events, is the almost insignificant black dot next to the Roman numeral II on the clock face at Horse Guards Parade. This marks and commemorates the exact hour of his execution.

L IS FOR:

Dr David **Livingstone** – was the Scottish explorer and missionary famous for his African expeditions, during which he discovered the Victoria Falls, Lakes Ngami, Malawi and parts of the Zambezi, in his elusive attempts to find the source of the River Nile.

It was during his fourth and final expedition that he had his famous encounter with Henry Stanley, who had been sent out to Africa, by the Royal Geographic Society who were concerned by the explorer's five-year absence and whereabouts. The two parties finaly met on the shores of Lake Ujiji, which was where Mr Stanley provided us with the immortal catch phrase, "Dr Livingston, I presume?" Fortunately for everyone involved, Mr. Stanley's presumption proved correct and after a while, having exchanged pleasantries they both went their separate ways. Livingston continued his explorations, and Stanley, returned home, happy to report that the intrepid explorer was alive and kicking, albeit not for much longer.

Royal Geographical Society Kensington Gore – T.B Huxley-Jones 1953

33

Two years after this famous encounter, Dr Livingstone died and his wish to have his heart buried in Africa was carried out, as it was buried in Ilala, Zambia, under the evocative sounding name of a mpundu tree. As for his body, this was embalmed, wrapped in bark and carried by his trusty servants for six hundred miles across land and sea, reaching Westminster Abbey, a mere thirteen months later, for its Christian burial.

Before this could take place, correct identification was needed, which fortunately was easily provided. First of all, there was his badly reset arm, crushed previously by a lion and secondly, there were the natives to consider, whom, having overcome their natural superstitions by carrying a dead body and risking life and limb in the process, were clear indicators, that this was indeed the missing man and missionary.

Dr Livingston's body was eventually buried in the centre of the Nave of Westminster Abbey, 18th May 1864 and lies under a stone slab inscribed with his merits. It also tells you that his heart was buried in the centre of Africa, 13th April 1863 at a place called Ulala, which should read as Ilala, but happens to be a spelling mistake.

As for the discovery of the source of the Nile, this was left to another Victorian explorer, John Hanning-Speke. He is commemorated by a grey granite obelisk deep within the much closer and safer bush of Kensington Gardens, a stone's throw away from Livingstone's statue at the Royal Geographical Society. His life incidentally, came to a very abrupt end, just hours before setting off for Bath, where he was due to give a lecture about his life and travels. Having decided to go out partridge shooting, he missed the bird and shot himself instead!

IS FOR:

Sir Thomas **More**, was the good friend, confidante and Lord Chancellor to Henry VIII whose high moral standards and staunch beliefs came between himself and the King. This resulted in Thomas ending his days up on the scaffold, on the orders of his former friend, after refusing to accept Henry's new religious policies, the life-changing Acts of Succession and Supremacy.

Their friend-ship began to go pear-shaped after the King announced his intentions to divorce his first wife, Catherine of Aragon, mother to 'Bloody Mary', in order to marry wife number two, Anne Boleyn, already pregnant with the future Queen Elizabeth. Awkward enough in itself, for Thomas to agree to, but when coupled with the subsequent and controversial Act of Succession, things really came to a head. Thomas, made his feelings known and Henry, not used to being disagreed with, ploughed on regardless. Anxious to marry with or without the consent of the Pope, which was not forthcoming, he then went one step further and introduced the Act of Supremacy. The first act meant that Elizabeth would have priority over Mary, in acceding to the throne, who would in turn, be declared illegitimate by this Act, and the second one, once in force would make Henry the new and supreme head of the Church of England, separating us from the Church of Rome and of course, the Pope. This had far-reaching affects and disastrous consequences for many sectors of society and in particular, for Thomas, who refused to swear the oath to Henry, and in opposing both acts, found himself guilty of High Treason.

Now most of this was to do with 'The Kings Great Matter', which, when simply boiled down, was Henry's pressing desire to have a son

35

and with all the component parts in place, a pregnant mistress and a discarded wife, he was all set for closure. The only obstacle blocking his future, was the Pope, without whose consent, he would be back in square one, which was the main reason for passing these Acts. Unfortunately, he also needed his friends' approval and when Thomas refused, Henry had him sent to the Tower of London, where he thought he would come to his senses, only he was proven wrong.

Fourteen months later, Thomas, obstinate as ever, showed no signs of remorse or changing his mind. His objections to Henry's constitutional and ecclesiastical changes stayed the same. Even his wife tried to intervene, remonstrating with her husband, "You've proved your point, just apologise and come home". It wasn't Thomas's style, "I'm the King's good servant, but God's first", he replied. Eventually, Henry's patience ran out and on 15th April 1534, Thomas was taken to Tower Hill and executed. Before the actual deed was done, he joked with the exectioner, asking for his help when mounting the scaffold, "At least I'll not be in need of it on the way down" and after kneeling into position, and adjusting his long and scraggy beard over the block, he stoked it fondly and added "T'would be a pity to cut this off, after all, it hasn't committed treason". Moments later, Sir Thomas More, was no more.

Afterwards, his body, minus its' severed head, was buried at St. Peter ad Vincula, the church within the Tower. The head was later taken over to London Bridge, where it was impaled upon a pole and displayed along with all the other decapitated heads of traitors. A common custom of the day, which provided an effective remedy, for would be perpetrators' against the Crown. The heads, resembling olives on toothpicks stayed in place, picked away at by birds, until all the flesh was removed and only the bare bones of their skulls remained.

Now one of Thomas's daughters, Margaret Roper, had no intention of leaving her father's head to decay in such a macabre way

and although distraught beyond belief, she hatched a daring plan. Together with an accomplice, they stole down to the bridge, in the middle of the night and whilst she waited, in a boat underneath it, her partner in crime scaled up the pole, upon which Thomas's head was attached, pulled it off and threw it over the side of the bridge. Luckily Margaret, who had already proved she was a good catch, being his married daughter, caught the head, stuffed it into a Hessian sack, and rowed down river to Canterbury.

On arrival, she made her way to St. Dunstan's Church, where her husband's family had their vault, and there, safe at last, she put her fathers' head to rest.

Chelsea Old Church, Chelsea Embankment – L Cubitt Bevis 1969

37

IS FOR:

Nelson

The uncle of Vice Admiral, Horatio, Viscount Nelson, was completely baffled by the family's decision to dispatch his twelve year old, sea faring nephew, off to sea and on hearing the news, demanded to know "What on earth has poor Horatio done, to deserve this?"

Little did he, or anyone, for that matter know, that his nephew would rapidly rise through the ranks, becoming a Vice Admiral and England's most famous naval hero. Which he did most spectacularly on 21st October 1805, and after giving the fleet the famous flagged signal "England expects every man will do his duty" he lead them into his final, decisive and victorious battle against the might of Napoleon.

This was the famous battle of Trafalgar, which proved to be a double edged-sword for Nelson, as although he won the battle, he also lost his life, falling prey to a bullet and a sharp shooting French sniper. Whose perfect aim fatally wounded Horatio, who, had been standing proudly on deck, clearly visible, in his bright crimson, full dress uniform. He fell to the deck and in his dying moments, was comforted by his Captain. As he lay in his arms, he uttered his final words, which were not "Kiss me Hardy" as commonly presumed, but the more serious ones, "Thank God I have done my duty", after which he died. The bullet, which caused the damage, was saved after being removed from his body, and is now on view within the State Apartments at Windsor Castle – a national treasure.

Now, normally deaths at sea were dealt with by sea-burials, but as Nelson had always hated the sea and the many bouts of seasickness caused by it, this was clearly out of the question. So, instead, he was

Trafalgar Square – EH Bailey 1834, the column by William Railton prepared for a homeward voyage within his own coffin, which he always travelled with, made out of English Oak.

At this stage, he became the envy of the entire fleet, as after his

body had been placed inside the coffin, he was totally submersed in the Navy's finest rum, used abundantly, on this occasion to preserve, rather than inebriate the body. He was then despatched off to England, arriving on our shores well and truly pickled, after a brief stopover in Gibraltar where a similar procedure took place involving more alcohol and a second coffin.

Nelson's funeral took place at St. Paul's Cathedral, where he is also buried, in the most prestigious of places. Right in its centre, directly under the dome and down in the crypt. His two coffins were put into an amazing black sarcophagus, on top of which is a carved purple cushion, which supports his coronet. However, this was never intended for Lord Nelson, as it had originally been built to accommodate Henry VIII's disgraced and former Chancellor, Cardinal Wolsey. The story goes, that after his fall from grace, the sarcophagus had been put into storage at Windsor Castle, where, until Nelson's death, it had remained, for the best of 275 years, redundant. Finally, now that a worthy occupant had arrived, it was rescued from obscurity, cleaned up and customised for the Admiral. The only alteration required being the removal of Wolsey's mitre, which made way for Nelson's last honour, his Viscount's coronet.

After his death, all his honours and titles passed to his brother, a country parson. The authorities, at the time, overlooked his wishes for them to be passed on his mistress, Emma Hamilton's daughter, the illegitimate Horatia. Both of who, after his death, lived a life of penury, and Emma, eventually died penniless in France, after being imprisoned for debt. Before all this, however, she and Lord Nelson had indulged in a very public affair, him having set-a-side his wife Fanny, in favour of her. The couple met out in Naples, where she and her husband, William, the British Ambassador, were living at time. Emma, aged thirty, and half her husbands age, soon found her self rather enamoured with the Admiral, who in the course of their duty, had been invited for dinner, on more than one occasion. Which is how and where their affair first began.

Once back in London, it raged on and became the talk of the town. So, in order to continue their romance more discreetly, they resorted to using remote and off the beaten track venues such as the Gun Pub in Blackwall. An idea location for illicit rendezvous', and where, in the privacy of a private room, hired especially for the occasion, the Admiral apparently serenaded her on his guitar – one can only presume this was long before he lost his right arm!

IS FOR:

William of **Orange** – was the asthmatic, hunch-backed, hook-nosed King from Holland, who ruled the country in joint sovereignty, with his wife Queen Mary. Both were direct descendents of King Charles I,

St James's Square – Sir John Bacon

being his grandchildren and therefore had equal rights to the throne and from whom we have inherited the expression, 'Going Dutch' from, ie to share equally, which is exactly was they both did.

41

Eleven years into their marriage, William was approached by Parliament, whom fed up with the existing Catholic King James II, asked him to assist them, with his overthrow. The idea went according to plan, James fled the country, famously, losing his jewels in the Wash and after agreeing to certain constitutional changes William and Mary were crowned joint monarchs.

This period in history is referred to as The Glorious Revolution, i.e. more power to Parliament and less to the monarchy, and whilst Parliament and the new King and Queen were all for it, the public, not at all keen on the new Dutch intrusion, put their feelings into rhyme and came up with the following ditty. It is now part of a well known nursery rhyme, and was not intended to flatter:

Hark, hark, the dogs do bark, the beggars are coming to town,
Some in rags and some in tags, and others in velvet gowns

The royal couple ignored these public sentiments and soon settled down to their adopted country and their own lifestyles. Queen Mary, happy to have moved away from the dank, damp palace in Whitehall and into the newly refurbished one in Kensington, soon set about re-organising the gardens and collecting her Blue and White China. Whilst William, when not out of the country, fighting the French, preferred the more rural delights of Hampton Court Palace, with his friends, especially the Duke of Albermarle. It was down there, that he had his fatal accident, caused by his horse tripping and stumbling on a molehill. William was thrown to the ground, broke his collarbone and died shortly thereafter, from pneumonia.

Far from being upset by this accident, it was celebrated with great glee by the Jacobites, the supporters of the recently deposed King James, who believed William to be a usurper to the throne. They therefore took great delight in drinking a toast to 'The little Gentleman with the black velvet waistcoat' a direct reference to the mole who had literally brought the House of Orange down, and the reason for depicting a molehill on William's equestrian statue.

P IS FOR:

Viscount **Palmerston** (the 3rd) Henry John Temple, had the longest career in Parliament, starting at the age of 26, as a Tory MP, until he was finally rewarded for his efforts, aged 70, when he became Prime Minister. During this lengthy career, he played an active part in furthering factory legislation and prison reform on the home front and abroad by concluding the Crimean War and suppressing the Indian Mutiny.

Parliament Square – Thomas Woolner

43

Despite being so busy, the Palmeston's were very sociable and greatly sought after on the dinner party circuit, however, they were also consistently late, always missing out on the first course, which was soup. One host, obviously irked by this lateness, went to great lengths one evening and took Lady Palmeston aside, produced a soup ladle and explained it basic use and functions! Apart from this slight faux pas, they were a very popular couple, especially Lord Palmeston, who was known as Pam by his friends and Cupid by the press, on account of his popularity with the ladies. By all accounts, he was a man of great charm, which mixed with power, money and a title, became an intoxicating cocktail for those who were interested and meant he really couldn't go far wrong, despite the fact he had a stoop, slight limp and wore the worse pair of false teeth ever fitted!

This ability of his to admire the opposite sex, landed him in hot water and earned him his tabloid nickname during his second term in office as Prime Minister, when he was accused of adultery with an Irish journalist's wife. The lady in question, a Mrs O'Kane alleged that he had used his offices for their liaisons. Fortunately for him, it all turned out to be a hoax, made all the more amusing by his age and the outcome, which instead of harming the elderly statesman's reputation, made him all the more popular!

Riding on the crest of this unexpected wave of popularity, he called for a general election, which, despite all odds, and pushing nearly eighty, he won. However, before parliament could reassemble he died, from a chill, after blatantly ignoring his doctors' advice to stay at home and nurse his cold. Fed up with looking at his four walls, he decided to take a ride around town in his open-topped carriage, his parting words being, "Die Doctor? That's the last thing I shall do!"

IS FOR:

The barren **Queen Anne** succeeded to the throne in 1702 after her brother-in-law, King William died, ruling the country for just twelve years, until she died from a fit of apoplexy brought on, after a serious binge of over-eating in 1714!

Food and drink had become her main solace, which is not hugely surprising, given her many illnesses and failed pregnancies, which numbered an astonishing eighteen in total. However despite her personal problems, she was a relatively decent Queen, keen on keeping a moral court and nation, achieved by issuing important proclamations, against indecency and vice and less important ones, against bad behaviour in the Royal Parks. Which meant that menials were banned from walking on the grass and disorderly people, beggars and rude boys were refused admittance.

Her personal life however, was something else. She was married to the bland, blond Prince George of Denmark, who was considered to be the dullest man at court. A man, deemed to be so boring, that when he fell asleep at the dinner table, as he frequently did, the witty courtiers would ask one another in mock horror "Has he died?" "No" would come the answer, "He's just asleep, but what's the difference!" He was also the reason, if folklore is to be believed, for their barren marriage, which came about after a trip to Ireland. George, was also known for his malicious streak of arrogance and impatience, which came to the fore, when travelling through the back roads of Ireland. His carriage was forced to pull up, due to a group of gypsies blocking the way and rather than wait for them to pass, he ordered his driver to continue on through, narrowly missing one of them. The story goes, that this gypsy,

45

put a curse on him, his wife and any subsequent heirs, which seemed to come to pass, as none of Queen Anne's baby's survived infancy.

Another source of unhappiness in her life was her very close friendship with Sarah, the Duchess of Marlborough, a friendship that ultimately led, as they can do, to contempt. The two ladies were neighbours, who, both living in St. James's frequently visited one another, with more or less free access and without the usual pomp. They even gave each other pet names and became Mrs Morley and Mrs Freeman. This informal arrangement caused the odd raised eyebrow, but

Queen Anne's Gate – unknown sculptor

it remained strong, up until the time of their famous row, caused, thought the Duchess, by the Queen who kept her waiting, "Like some Scottish woman with a petition!" Their quarrel was never patched up and the Queen literally died, before seeing her old friend again.

Back as court, it was a different matter again, as far as manners went, which even then, were considered rather shocking, by all the frequent bouts of belching, burping and other indiscriminate noises, which made their unwelcome presence known. A poet of the time, was the cheeky Tom D'Urfrey, who drew extra attention to this, with his satirical poem, succinctly entitled *The Fart* which literally swept through the court amusing many, as the main culprit, as this first verse states, was none other than the Queen:

When at Noon, as in State, The Queen was at Meat
And the Princely Dane sat by her
A fart there was heard, that the company scared
As a Gun at their Ears had been fired.

The blame finally and usually landed on the Yeoman of the Guard, innocently standing outside the dining-room and therefore finished off with:

But the Truth of the Sound, not at all could be found
Since none by the doer could tell
So to hush up the shame, The Beef-eater bore the blame
And the Queen, God be praised, dined well.

Of the two statues of Queen Anne, the one pictured here is in Queen Anne's Gate, and unlike the other one which is in front of St. Paul's Cathedral, this one, apparently is a phantom, who, on the anniversary of her death, 1st August, gets down from its plinth and takes itself off for a walk!

R IS FOR:

Richard I, le Coeur de Lion, was, in plain old English, Richard the Lionheart, famous for his crusades, his short reign and the lack of time he spent in the country.

He was very much the blue-eyed boy, being the adored and doted on son of Eleanor of Aquitaine, who, after being left by her husband, King

Henry II in favour of 'Sweet Rosalind', also decided to leave England. So she went off to live in France with her boy Richard, whom she continued to prime for his eventual role as King of England.

Disillusioned with her husband and his despotic ways she turned her entire attention onto her boys, whom were encouraged, at every opportunity to rebel against their father. A plan which slightly backfired with her imprisonment. However, after his death and her release, her plans came to fruition, as both Richard and John succeeded in turn to the throne. Being spoilt boys, neither of them made great Kings, especially Richard, who spent just a few months in the county. The one and only memorable occasion of his reign being the time he denounced London, declaring, "If I could only find a buyer, I'd sell it", after which, he left once again, that time, for good.

His mother pretty much took care of everything for him, even down to finding him a bride. The lady chosen for this role was the gentle and

48

Old Palace Yard – Baron Carlo Marochetti

submissive Berengaria of Navarre, whose wooden effigy is exhibited at the Victoria and Albert Museum, together with the other effigies of members of the Plantagenet family. She was the perfect choice for Richard as she never objected to anything he said or did, mainly because he was absent from the very start. This pattern of behaviour began at their wedding, which took place in Cyprus, during a hard earned break away from the thrilling world of Crusades. It was a unique wedding, made all the more unusual by the groom whose chose not to attend, but sent along his sword instead, to which, by way of proxy, the lovely Beregaria was married!

As Richard's whole life was spent in combat, it was no huge surprise that he died that way, sword in hand and during an attack on a French castle. The fatal blow was delivered accidentally, by the archer Bertrand de Gourdon, who was later called on, to explain his actions to the King, then laid out on his deathbed. This scene of the dying King

remonstrating with the archer is clearly depicted on the base of the plinth, which supports his statue, and as it took Richard all of twelve days to die, there was plenty of time for reflection and recrimination.

As for his statue, this was sculpted by the exuberant Baron Carlo Marochetti and occupies Old Palace Yard, now the exclusive car park for members of the House of Lords. It shows King Richard looking pretty impressive on his horse, and holding his sword, through which, we have come to define him, raised defiantly in the air. This, however, experienced a slight hick-up during World War II, when the strong reverberations of a nearby bomb blast, adversely affected its tip, which ended up like its owner – bent!

49

S IS FOR:

Sarah Siddons – was the leading actress of her day, whose talent, capacity and knack for mesmerising and captivating her audiences of theatregoers and critics, established her as 'The Supreme Queen of Tragedy, Pain and Sadness'. It was a well-deserved accolade for this actress whose performances at the Theatre Royal, Drury Lane were legendary, particularly her portrayal of Lady Macbeth, which became her speciality

Sarah was the oldest of twelve children, born into a family of travelling actors, who thought it best she broke with family tradition in

Paddington Green – Leon-Joseph Chavalliaud 1897

favour of a more secure job in service. So she was sent off to work as a maid in a respectable household, where, try as she might to suppress her natural talents and abilities, in favour of her unnatural ones as a maid, she simply couldn't, and took to entertaining her employers and their dinner guests with impromptu and unsolicited performances. Enjoyable, as this was for a while, the novelty of an in-house actress cum maid soon wore off and they eventually parted company. Sarah continued the family tradition and went on to achieve great fame by treading the boards, and the family continued theirs, by dining in peace.

Her career blossomed, as did her fame, so in order to capture this beauty on canvas, Thomas Gainsborough, the top portrait painter of the day was commissioned. He, however, was far from impressed with the actress, on account of her long nose, and his inability to portray it. After several unsuccessful attempts, with tempers running high, Gainsborough, madly frustrated, was reported to have completely lost his, and in a fit of pique, threw down his long brushes down, and swore, ""Damn the nose, is there no end to it?"

Another detractor of hers' was the poet and Greek supporter, Lord Bryon, who turned out to have equally strong opinions about Sarah, which on reflection were not at all flattering. He simply couldn't see what all the fuss was about, and declared her to have no sex appeal whatsoever, then indorsed his opinion, by saying he would sooner sleep with the Archbishop of Canterbury, definitely a man ahead of his time!

Sarah is buried at St. Mary's, Paddington Green and this statue of her, which portrays her as a tragic muse overlooks the Westway, which leads eastwards towards Baker Street, where her former home was situated. This has since become the Lost Property Office for London Transport, an ironic touch as she too, was extremely forgetful!

T IS FOR:

William Tyndale – was one of the early supporters of the Reformation, which back in the 1520's made him a controversial figure, who ended up paying for his beliefs with his life. Sad to say, he was one step ahead of his time and because of his work, outlook and views, he became alienated from the church whom, feeling threatened, by him, labelled him as public enemy No. 1.

This man was totally dedicated to his work, and unshakeable in his belief that the word of God should be made freely and readily available to all, i.e. in English rather than Greek. Which was therefore only understood by members of the clergy, unlike the masses who didn't'. Because of this great dividing line, they were therefore able to exert massive control over their congregations, who, being unfamiliar with the language never questioned it. But, now, with Tyndale, about to blow their cover, and provide an English

52

Victoria Embankment Gardens – Boehm 1884

translation to these hidden mysteries, the clergy realised they were about to loose their control and relinquish their stronghold. As far as the Church was concerned, this was not an option, and by way of stopping, or at least delaying this disastrous sequence of events, which turned out

to be just around the corner, they branded him a traitor and his work a treasonable offence.

He had already begun translating the New Testament, but before it was completed, he was forced to leave the country, so he moved abroad to Germany, where, exiled in the city of Worms and encouraged by his friends Erasmus and Luther, he finished it off.

Once this was completed and the Good Word started filtering through, he was forced to move once again. This time it was over to Antwerp, where his attempts to start unravelling and translating the Old Testament were thwarted, as he was soon betrayed and arrested.

He died, a martyr to his cause, in the Castle of Vilvorde after being seized, strangled and then burnt at the stake. His work however was 'miraculously' saved and Tyndale's final prayer was also answered. Having prayed, "Lord, open the King of England's Eyes", they were, and one year after his death, the English Bible was, as he had intended, freely, readily and available to all.

53

V IS FOR:

Queen Victoria is eagerly awaited birth came as a great relief, not only to her parents but also the monarchy, which almost come unstuck due to the embarrassing lack of legitimate heirs. The story behind her birth is a fairly unusual one, and as she was born out of necessity and ambition rather than love, it makes a good one.

Her predecessors were King George IV and William IV, who she referred to, as her 'wicked uncles'. They unfortunately, had seen all their legitimate heirs die before themselves and although William's had died in infancy, it was a big shock when Charlotte, George's only daughter, unexpectedly died in childbirth, together with her baby. Hence the gaping hole, a new opportunity and a race amongst their other ageing brothers to produce the next King or Queen of England.

As most of these chaps led debased and decadent lives, estranged from their wives and living with their mistresses, it made the whole process rather amusing, when these elderly Dukes found themselves recalled and for the sole purpose of procreation, forced to reacquaint themselves with their spouses. Victoria's parents, the Duke and Duchess of Kent, were definitely in this category having been estranged from one another for some time. The Duke, madly in debt, and forced to live abroad, had been enjoying life with his mistress Madame du Laurent, which suddenly came to an abrupt end when he was summons home and like his other brothers, required to get down to the unpleasant business of thinking about England.

Nine months later, he was rewarded with the birth of his daughter, the future Queen of England, who was christened Alexandrina Victoria and nine months after that, exhausted by

Kensington Gardens – Princess Louise

events, he died, leaving his wife to bring her up.

Her mother was extremely strict, and life at Kensington Palace

was rather tedious, relieved, it transpires by her unbecoming behaviour. Bellowing at the servants was one way of relieving the boredom and another way, which never failed, was annoying her mother by her appalling table manners. Once she became Queen, she wrote, how on one occasion, she was forced to remind her mother who she now was, which really indicated her true feelings for her! Just after her eighteenth birthday, following the death of her uncle, King William, she became Queen and reigned for the next sixty-three years, thus becoming our longest reigning monarch to date. She proposed to her cousin Albert, married him, moved out of Kensington, and into Buckingham Palace, where she proceeded to rule the country and

55

give birth. They had nine children in quick succession, which was all brought to a grinding halt by Albert's premature death, caused by typhoid fever, after which a life of self-inflicted mourning followed for almost the rest of her reign. This, together with her alleged quotes, black outfits and reclusive lifestyle became almost as tedious as her earlier years at Kensington Palace, which is where we will go back to, in order to see what she looked like, just starting out at the beginning of her reign.

This statue, on view at the side of the palace, is in front of the room in which she was born, (now open to the paying public) and was sculpted by one of her daughters, Princess Louse, the 'arty' one of the family. She, in her day, was a bit of a loose canon, whose habit for taking up with the wrong sort of man, had given her quite a reputation, so in order to rectify this, she was married off to the Marquis of Lorne. This turned out to be another mistake, as he too, had a similar reputation and preference, which was about the only thing they both had in common! After parting company, he disappeared off to France and she went back to the family home, and took up sculpture for a hobby. Her tutor was the much respected and revered Sir Edgar Boehm, who gave her expert tutelage and guidance in sculpture and also took the time, to indulge in a spot of extra curriculum activity. It was during the later, that things took a turn for the worse, when during one of their lovemaking sessions, down at his Fulham studios, he had a heart attack and died. Princess Louise vehemently denied any involvement whatsoever, and maintained that the cause of his attack had merely been brought on after moving a heavy bust!

W IS FOR:

Oscar Final O'Flahertie Wills **Wilde** was the Irish play-write, wit and super-star, who enjoyed exposing the social hypocrisy of his day through his plays such as *Lady Windermere's Fan*, *An Ideal Husband* and *The Importance of Being Earnest*. All of which stand the test of time, but ultimately highlighted the world into which he aspired, was accepted and then rejected. Intent on making a name for himself, he started attracting notoriety, starting in his early days at Magdelene College, Oxford, where he kept a pet lobster and an impressive collection of Blue and White China. This obviously annoyed his fellow students intently, as they not only smashed his china but also boiled the lobster! After Oxford came London, where he became even more outrageous, with his outlandish behaviour. On one occasion he attracted more attention than usual by walking up and down Piccadilly wearing a rather loud suit and carrying a sunflower to boot. By now, he was already the talk of the town, which was fine by him, after all, according

to Oscar, the only thing worse than being talked about, was not being talked out about at all, which for him, was easily achieved, not only by his comments, ways and wit, but also by his unconventional lifestyle. His marriage to Constance, two sons and life in Chelsea

57

The Strand – Maggie Hambling, unveiled by his grandson Merlin Holland and his son Lucian

being somewhat at odds with his tempestuous love affair, with Alfred 'Bosie" Douglas, whom he had fallen madly and passionately in love with. None of this, of course, sat too well with Alfred's dad, the formidable Marquis of Queensberry, known as 'Q' who had many a run-in with his son's lover, whom he hurtled abuse and rotting flowers at, in an attempt to break up their union. This included using the strange word 'Sondermite', as he was clearly unfamiliar with the correct pronunciation. The whole affair fell dramatically apart, and Oscar was accused of the illegal act of homosexuality. He soon found himself in the dock and unsuccessful in his self-defence, was pronounced guilty by the jury and sentenced to two-years imprisonment. He was arrested at the Cadogan Hotel, by local policemen, whose accent and consideration for the other residents was perfectly summed up in Sir John Betjeman's ditty:

Sir, we have come to arrest you, to take you where prisoners do dwell
Please assist us and come quitely, as this is The Cadogan Hotel

The two years of hard labour at Reading Goal nearly finished him off, after which, released in body but reduced in health and mind, he headed for Paris, where living anonymously under the name of Sebastian Melmouth he stayed until he died. His time in prison wasn't a complete waste, as it was there that he wrote his famous *Ballad of Reading Goal*, which despite the title, is the most exquisitely, beautifully written work.

Being the master of the one-liners, Oscar's last words were about as good as they get. Aesthetically minded to the end, lying and now dying in his dingily decorated, puce coloured room, he left us with his last pronouncement, "Either the wallpaper goes, or I do".

IS FOR:

Eleanor's **Cross** – The Eleanor Cross commemorates the life of the medieval Queen Eleanor of Castile, the wife of Edward I, who died in 1290, and shows her represented by eight little statues, four of which depict her as a Queen and the other four as a Christian.

Originally there were twelve crosses, which were erected in her memory, after she died in childbirth up in Hadby, Northamptonshire. Each one was erected on the spot that her coffin rested overnight on its twelve day journey south to London. Nowadays, only three remain and this one in London is a Victorian replica, put up in 1865 replacing the medieval one, destroyed by Cromwell's men.

59

Charing Cross Station Forecourt – AS Barry and Thomas Earp

The story of Eleanor and Edward is one of love, a rarity within many Royal marriages, and unique within arranged ones, which this one was, having been put together, by his father, King Henry III and her brother Alphonso of Castile, for the usual profitable reasons. Contrary, to the norm, it turned out to be a roaring success, as it was love at first sight for these young teenagers, and having fallen madly in love with one another, they were inseparable throughout their marriage. She even accompanied him on crusade, unheard of, in that day and age, which was just as well, as during their travels her love for him was really put to the test.

At the time, the King, having hammered the Scots, annoyed the Welsh and expelled the Jews, was keen to make his presence felt in another part of the world, hence the crusade. When, he unwittingly attracted the undesirable attentions of a poisoned arrow, which alighted, unfortunately, on a very sensitive and vulnerable spot. The King, writhing around in agony on the ground, having fallen from his horse, felt the unwelcome poison spreading through his body and knew he wasn't long for this world. At which point, the lovely Eleanor, leapt off her horse and into action. Kneeling down, beside her husband, she exceeded her brief and went beyond the normal wifely duty, in affirming her affection for him, by sucking all the poison out, and therby saving his life – she was a very dedicated wife!

These crosses, therefore, are a fitting tribute to her from him, especially the one in London, which now sits on the forecourt of Charing Cross station, a mainline commuter railway terminus. This also takes her name as the word Charing derives from the French, La Chere Reine, which in Eleanor's time was the language of the court and also her pet name, the Darling Queen, who came from Spain!

Y IS FOR:

Duke of **York** – was the Grand one, whom, according to the nursery rhyme, marched his men up a hill and then marched them down again, but in real life was Frederick Augustus, Duke of York and Albany, the second son of King George III.

He was also the Commander-in-Chief of the British armed forces, a responsible role, which earned him the respect of all his men, who ended up contributing a days pay towards his column and statue.

After his death, the wags of the day put forward the suggestion that he, now way up on his column, he was finally and completely out

The Mall – Sir Richard Westmacott 1834

61

of reach from his creditors, who although were not the reason for his death, took the blame.

The Duke, like so many of his brothers, possessed a lethal roving eye, which had caused him a bit of grief in an earlier liaison, with a lady called Mary Anne Clarke, whom for professional reasons he was forced to give the heave-ho to. It transpired that she had been selling army commissions on the black market to dubious individuals, which given his position, being head of the armed forces, was not ideal. So, with Mrs. Clarke now out of out of the way, a vacancy presented itself, which was quickly filled by his neighbour, the Duchess of Rutland.

She and her husband lived just of St. James's Street, in Rutland House, nowadays, The Royal Overseas Club. This overlooks Green Park, one of London's Royal parks, and as it turned out, was a very convenient place for the lovers to meet. The fact that it was so close to home was of little consequence to these two, whose afternoon canoodling sessions were often interrupted by passers-by. The only person unaware of these shenanigans, it seemed, was her husband, whom in typical British tradition employed a stiff upper lip and a blind eye, until, its' alleged, his wife's death.

Shortly after her demise, the Duke of York, was invited up to Rutland House, by the Duke of Rutland, for drinks. York, somewhat surprised by the invitation, duly accepted it and presented himself at the appointed hour. He was shown into the library, which overlooks the afore-mentioned park and offered a drink. One sip later, he fell stone dead to the floor! The cause of his death was put down to a heart attack, brought on, it was explained by him hearing his creditors banging at the door, however, it remains one of historys unsolved mysteries – was it the sweet wine, or was it even sweeter revenge?

Z

IS FOR:

The **Zimbabwe** House Nudes caused a huge sensation and public outcry, which was backed and fuelled by the national newspapers, when they were unveiled in 1907. The occupants at the time were the British Medical Association, who decided to advertise themselves and their profession by decorating the outside of their newly acquired offices. For this task they commissioned the eminent sculptor, Jacob Epstein, who

63

The Strand – Jacob Epstein

carried out Charles Holden's designs and sculpted eighteen nudes, all of which perfectly represented the *Ages of Man*.

Nowadays, their mutilated state is a far cry from how they once looked, which makes it all the harder to understand why the public and the newspapers reacted so strongly to them at the time. The papers, informed the public to be extra vigilant when approaching the Strand and went on to warn fathers to shield the eyes of their children and young men to take great care of their fiancés!

Meanwhile, across the road and up on the second floor offices occupied by a Biblical Association it was altogether a different matter and by way of protecting their employees from this unwelcome view, they went one step further than the newspapers had, and immediately changed all their windows from clear glass to frosted!

However, as soon as the public reaction had died down, it was then Nature's turn, who, stepped in and single-handedly wreaked more havoc on these statues than ever imagined.

The problem arose because they had been sculpted from porous stone, which given our climate was not a good idea, as over time, they had absorbed copious amounts of rainwater, which in due course had turned to frost. This resulted in the natural and unwelcome phenomenon of expansion and cracking, which, is never good for nudes! Especially in this case, when a falling phallus dropped without warning, narrowly missing a passer-by!

It apparently missed him by a hair's breadth, which was lucky for him but not for the statues, which were now deemed to be a public risk as well as menace. The authorities, glad to have a legitimate excuse, to make them 'safer', took immediate action and began their remedial work. Hours later and before you could even say 'Jack Frost', the workmen had rendered the entire *Ages of Man* unrecognisable, by having had all their loose appendages hacked away and offensive protruberences chopped off!